D1197776

MYSTERY EXPLORERS™

SEARCHING FOR

BIGFOOT

rosen publishing's
rosen
central®

New York

Stew

an

Published in 2012 by The Rosen Publishing Group, Inc.
29 East 21st Street, New York, NY 10010

Copyright © 2012 by The Rosen Publishing Group, Inc.

First Edition

All rights reserved. No part of this book may be reproduced in any form without permission in writing from the publisher, except by a reviewer.

Library of Congress Cataloging-in-Publication Data

Cowley, Stewart.
Searching for Bigfoot/Stewart O. Cowley, Greg Cox.—1st ed.
    p. cm.—(Mystery explorers)
Includes bibliographical references and index.
ISBN 978-1-4488-4760-0 (library binding)—
ISBN 978-1-4488-4768-6 (pbk.)—
ISBN 978-1-4488-4776-1 (6-pack)
1. Sasquatch—Juvenile literature. I. Cox, Greg, 1959– II. Title.
QL89.2.S2C686 2012
001.944—dc22

                                                                2011000531

Manufactured in the United States of America

CPSIA Compliance Information: Batch #S11YA: For further information, contact Rosen Publishing, New York, New York, at 1-800-237-9932.

CONTENTS

INTRODUCTION

Something is lurking in the depths of the primeval forest—a large, ape-like creature, more than 7 feet (2.13 meters) tall, covered from head to toe with black hair or fur. The monster walks upright like a person, its massive arms swinging at its sides. It seems less like a bear or a gorilla than some sort of missing link between man and ape.

Its face is dark and hairless, with a flattened nose, and bony ridges jut out above its brown eyes. Thick, black hair covers its ears. A strong animal odor emanates from the beast-man, yet it maintains an eerie silence, emitting no grunts or roars. All it ever seems to leave behind—the only evidence of its existence—are a set of enormous footprints, each over 2 feet (0.6 m) long, pressed deeply into the dirt and mud.

Everyone has seen the grainy, super-8 film clip of a tall, hairy man-beast lumbering on two huge feet along a forest edge, barely pausing to cast a glance over its furry shoulder. Is this really the creature now known inter-changeably as Bigfoot or Sasquatch—a mysterious survivor of a previously unknown race of giant primates—or some misapprehended projection of our own primal fears? Is Bigfoot a manifestation of modern humans' need to believe in something primeval and untouched by civilization still lurking out there, or is it all a giant hoax?

No matter what one's level of belief or skepticism in the phenomenon, it's an undeniably entertaining saga, incorporating mythology, folklore, adventure, exploration, crackpot theories, elaborate frauds, and genuine scientific investigation. This book lays all of this out in rich and savory detail, from anthropological evidence and Native American mythology to primary source documents and travelers' tales, urban legends, and pop culture artifacts.

What is out there? Whether the creature known as Bigfoot really exists, is an elaborate fraud, or is simply wishful thinking has been the subject of debate for more than a hundred years and is likely to continue to be so for many more.

CHAPTER 1

Scientific Approaches to Bigfoot

U nlike ghosts or fairies, there is nothing in modern science that precludes, or argues against, the existence of creatures such as Bigfoot. Large simians like gorillas, chimpanzees, gibbons, and orangutans inhabit the Earth. In biology, these advanced primates are called hominoids, a category that also includes humans, or *Homo sapiens*. At one time, the African mountain gorilla was regarded as a myth, until science proved its actual existence. Why couldn't there be large, hairy hominoids in North America as well?

The Biology of Bigfoot

Bigfoot is typically described as a large, heavy anthropoid

6

Associate professor of zoology Angelo Capparella, of Illinois State University, examines hair samples said to belong to Bigfoot. These samples were collected during the first Bigfoot expedition ever to use rigorous scientific methodology.

anywhere from 7 to 10 feet (2 to 3 m) tall. Broad-shouldered, with a wide torso and very little neck, an adult Bigfoot may weigh as much as 800 or 900 pounds (363 to 408 kilograms), judging from the depths to which the mysterious footprints sink. Aside from their faces, hands, and feet, their bodies are almost completely carpeted with thick hair or fur. They appear to wear no clothing and possess no tools or other artifacts, aside from simple stones that they sometimes hurl at intruders.

Bigfoot hair is usually black or reddish-brown, although there were several sightings of a white-haired Bigfoot in the 1950s and '60s. Possibly this was a single specimen of an albino Sasquatch that has since died. Grover Krantz of Washington State University, one of the few qualified scientists to make a serious study of the subject, estimates that the average life span of a Bigfoot is about forty years, which would certainly explain the disappearance of the rare white Bigfoot.

Some Native American legends describe Sasquatch as a fierce man-eater, but this seems more folklore than fact. According to witnesses, Bigfoot has a wide and varied diet, including wild berries, nuts, roots, pine needles, and the occasional rodent or rabbit. It is also thought to dig for clams, strip the leaves from willow bushes, and wade into cold mountain streams in search of salmon. In addition, Bigfoot has sometimes been accused of stealing fish, chickens, and fresh fruit from campsites as well as from isolated farms and residences. Some experts believe that Bigfoot is also capable of snaring wild deer and elk with its bare hands, but the evidence for this is sketchier. Based on these theories and reports, it would seem that Bigfoot is an omnivore, meaning that the creature subsists on both meat and plants.

Unlike all other current primates except humans, Bigfoot is said to be bipedal, meaning that it walks erect on two legs. If true, this means that the discovery of an actual, living Bigfoot could teach us much about the evolution of the human species. At present, most scientists believe that *Homo sapiens* (modern humans) are the only bipedal hominids to walk the Earth and have been ever since our prehistoric cousins, the Neanderthals, died off thirty thousand years ago. But what if they're wrong and humans still share the planet with some kind of primitive ape-man—a missing link or an evolutionary offshoot that became a dead end?

The Fossil Record: *Gigantopithecus*

The fossil record proves that all sorts of human-sized primates have walked the Earth in the past, many of them even more humanlike than the great apes of today. Scientists keep digging up the remains of different types of early humans, some of them over four million years old. These are called hominids, a biological family that includes us as well as all of our supposedly extinct human ancestors. Throughout prehistory, at least fourteen different varieties of hominid have roamed free; *Homo sapiens* have only had the world to themselves for the last thirty thousand years. Or have we?

Some experts believe that we have already met Bigfoot in the fossil record, and that the mystery monster is actually one of our prehistoric cousins and not really extinct after all. A prime candidate is *Gigantopithecus blacki*, an ancient primate whose jawbones and teeth have been found in both China, Vietnam, and India. This creature had two close relatives found mostly in India, *Gigantopithecus bilaspurensis* and *Gigantopithecus giganteus*.

As its name suggests, *Gigantopithecus* was as tall as—or even taller than—Bigfoot is said to be and fits the standard description of a Sasquatch very closely. This towering creature, the largest primate to ever dwell upon the Earth, may have been as much as 10 feet (3 m) tall and weigh 1,200 pounds (540 kg). Females were considerably smaller. *Gigantopithecus* is believed by some authorities to have walked erect on two legs, just like

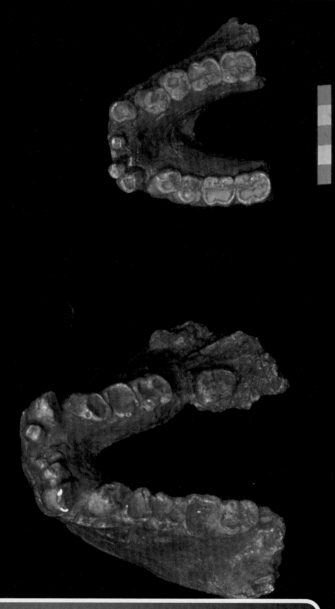

These fossilized jawbones of a *Gigantopithecus* were found in a Chinese cave in 1955. Some people believe they are the remains of a Yeren, the so-called Wild Man, a shaggy, red-haired ape-man.

Bigfoot does. "Giganto" lived as recently as five hundred thousand years ago and survived into the Pliocene ice age, when a land bridge connected Siberia to Alaska. It is possible that the creature emigrated from Asia to North America, where perhaps its descendants still live today.

If nothing else, the scientifically indisputable fact that *Gigantopithecus* once existed alongside our own primitive ancestors proves that a creature like Bigfoot is at least biologically possible. It should be noted, however, that *Gigantopithecus* fossils have never been found in the Americas. Because no *Gigantopithecus* bones or fossils have been discovered anywhere, there is no evidence to suggest that "Giganto" was bipedal. Indeed, some scientists believe that the creature's height and mass were so great that upright walking would have been nearly impossible. Most researchers believe the creature walked on all four limbs like chimpanzees and gorillas.

Many of these scientists also point out that the *Gigantopithecus* was not a hominin, meaning it did not occupy the evolutionary branch shared by humans, chimpanzees, and bonobos. This would seem to undercut the likelihood of it evolving over time into an upright, bipedal "man-ape."

Alternate Theory: *Paranthropus* and Bigfoot

A competing theory holds that Bigfoot is some species of *Paranthropus*, part of the *Australopithecus* line of primates believed to have lived in Africa 1.2 to 2 million years ago. *Paranthropus* had a bony ridge (called a sagittal crest) running along the top of its skull, providing extra support for its powerful jaw muscles.

THE BIGFOOT EXPERTS

When reading accounts of Bigfoot sightings and other supposed evidence, the opinions and conclusions of "experts" are often cited to support the argument for or against the creature's existence. But who are these experts, and what are their qualifications?

Grover Krantz (1931–2002) was the preeminent Bigfoot researcher, one whose academic credentials were impressive but who paid a heavy price for his investigations. He was a professor of physical anthropology at Washington State University and an expert in evolutionary anthropology and primatology (the study of primates). At first a Bigfoot skeptic, Krantz believed the Patterson-Gimlin footage of a large, hairy ape-man was a hoax. Yet upon studying the plaster casts made from tracks gathered in Bossburg, Washington, which seemed to indicate a club-footed Bigfoot, Krantz became a believer. He even came to accept the authenticity of the Patterson-Gimlin film. He was a champion of the theory that Bigfoot was descended from the Asian ape *Gigantopithecus*, which at some point must have crossed the land bridge across the Bering Strait into North America. Once converted to belief in Bigfoot, most of Krantz's academic work was devoted to Sasquatch research. This earned him the scorn of his peers, impeded his professional advancement, and restricted funding sources for his investigations. Most of his publications and articles on the subject were ignored or mocked by the academic world.

Another leading Bigfoot expert is cryptozoologist Loren Coleman. Cryptozoology is the study of animals that are legendary or whose existence has not yet been proved with biological evidence. Cryptozoology is not a recognized branch of zoology. Many people dismiss it as a pseudoscience, especially since it relies so heavily on unverified sightings, stories, and eyewitness accounts—rather than hard scientific data—for evidence. Coleman did study both anthropology and zoology. He taught at several universities before retiring to devote himself to writing on cryptozoology and the related fields of animal mysteries and folklore. Coleman also established the International Cryptozoology Museum in Portland, Maine. His fieldwork and writing have centered upon Native American traditions regarding Sasquatch, as well as sightings and evidence traces.

Though still often dismissed as "pseudo" or "fringe" science, some bright lights and highly respected authorities within the fields of zoology, primatology, and anthropology have begun to express academic interest in Bigfoot. Chimpanzee researcher and advocate Jane Goodall has expressed certainty that Bigfoot exists, and Jeffrey Meldrum, a professor of anthropology and anatomy at Idaho State University, has written academic papers evaluating Sasquatch footprints and the creature's bipedal movements.

The Bigfoot that appears in the infamous Patterson-Gimlin film also has such a crest, giving its head a pointed appearance. Various witnesses have also described Bigfoot's head as somewhat conical.

Paranthropus was considerably smaller than "Giganto," with males only about 4 feet (1.2 m) tall and 120 pounds (54 kg). Paranthropus had a hairy, stocky body with long arms, a gorilla-shaped head, and gorillalike molars for powerful chewing. It seems to have walked erect at least occasionally, like a human or a Sasquatch. Yet no Paranthropus fossils have ever been found outside of Africa, making the creature's theoretical migration to North America a problematic issue. Neither Giganto, nor Paranthropus, nor Bigfoot are known

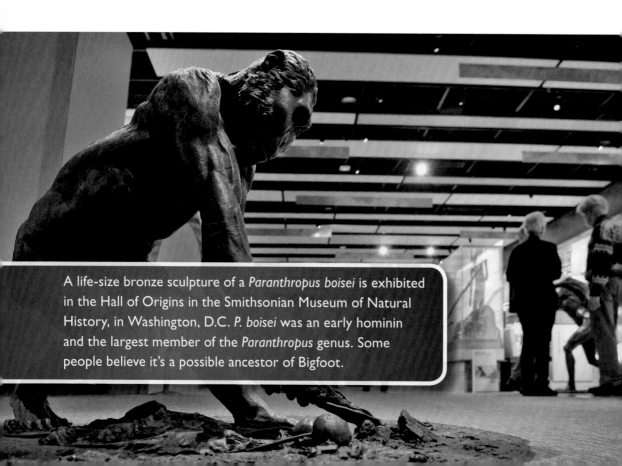

A life-size bronze sculpture of a *Paranthropus boisei* is exhibited in the Hall of Origins in the Smithsonian Museum of Natural History, in Washington, D.C. *P. boisei* was an early hominin and the largest member of the *Paranthropus* genus. Some people believe it's a possible ancestor of Bigfoot.

to have employed tools or fire, placing them at roughly the same level of cultural development.

A case can be made for either *Gigantopithecus* or *Paranthropus* being Bigfoot's true identity, but it is also possible that there is more than one kind of unknown hominid or hominoid roaming North America. Maybe both creatures still lurk in the primeval forests. Some people even argue that Bigfoot may be a surviving Neanderthal or *Homo erectus*, though there's no evidence that either ever existed in the Americas.

Perhaps Bigfoot is an entirely new species unknown to science. The answer remains hidden somewhere in the wilderness, beyond our present knowledge.

CHAPTER 2

EARLY ACCOUNTS OF SASQUATCH

Native American legends and folklore have long told of wild, hairy giants living deep in the forests of North America. Tales of frontier encounters with such creatures date back to at least the nineteenth century. Also known as Sasquatch, a name derived from similar terms used by a variety of Canadian Indian tribes, Bigfoot is an ongoing mystery, with new sightings being reported, and new tracks being discovered, on a regular basis.

Close Encounters

The prospect of accidentally running into an inhuman creature over 7 feet (2 m) tall is a frightening one, but how dangerous is Bigfoot? In most modern accounts of Bigfoot

The artist William M. Rebsamen depicted Bigfoot as a species of *Gigantopithecus* in this painting.

encounters, the creature appears more interested in avoiding humans than in attacking them, but there are older stories in which the Sasquatch behaves much more aggressively. It is possible that as humans and human settlements have encroached more upon Bigfoot's territory, the creatures have abandoned the fight and sought safety through seclusion.

A Canadian prospector named Albert Ostman repeatedly claimed to have been abducted and temporarily held hostage by an entire family of Sasquatches—a father, a mother, and two young children—back in 1924. Trapped in a remote valley near coastal British Columbia, Canada, he spent a couple of days observing the creatures, who mostly left him alone. He finally managed to escape by tricking the large male Bigfoot into trying some of the prospector's powdered tobacco. The noxious snuff made the creature so violently ill that Ostman was able to flee the valley during the resulting confusion.

The very same year, on Mount St. Helens in Washington State, another set of prospectors fought off a hostile band of enraged Bigfoots after the men shot (and possibly killed) a large, simian creature in what is now called Ape Canyon. The prospectors' log cabin was besieged at night by gorillalike "mountain devils" who shrieked and howled as they hurled heavy rocks at the walls and roof of the cabin. At one point during that terrifying evening, a hairy arm reached into the cabin through a chink in the wall, groping for an axe, before being repelled by gunfire. The frightened miners later described their attackers as having "the appearance of huge gorillas," their massive bodies covered all over with long black hair. They also found numerous footprints, roughly 2 feet (0.6 m) in length.

THE NAME OF THE BEAST

"Sasquatch" is not truly a Native American word for the giant, hairy, bipedal creature that is part of their folkloric tradition. Rather the word was coined by a Canadian newspaperman, J. W. Burns, who wrote a series of articles on the Native American tales of the giant forest-dwelling ape-man. He borrowed the Native American word *sesquac*, which means "wild man" and refers to a mythical or natural being that possesses a spirit better left alone. From this loan word, Burns created "Sasquatch."

The name "Bigfoot" was not invented until 1958, over three decades after the Ape Canyon incident. The word first appeared in the *Humboldt Times* of Eureka, California, in an article reporting on a construction worker's discovery of 16-inch (0.4 m) humanlike footprints. The whole notion of an unknown man-monster running around the Pacific Northwest did not really become widespread until national newspapers started covering the topic in the late-1950s. Nevertheless, a 1924 Oregon newspaper account of the Mount St. Helen's prospectors' bizarre story mentions that "Indians have told of the 'mountain devils' for 60 years," and that tracks such as the miners described "have been seen by forest rangers and prospectors for years." In other words, Bigfoot was haunting the forests long before he was given a name and became famous.

The Mystery of Jacko

In 1884, according to the *Victoria Daily Colonist*, a strange creature, "something of a gorilla type," was captured alongside a railroad near the village of Yale, in British Columbia. The hairy monster, nicknamed "Jacko," was apparently spying on a passenger train when people aboard the train spotted him. The train was stopped so that a number of the train's crew could chase after the creature. They eventually knocked Jacko unconscious with a rock, tied him up with a heavy rope, and then shipped him to Yale.

Jacko was watched over by a Yale resident named George Tilbury. The creature remained largely silent but occasionally emitted a sound that was described as half-growl and half-bark. He ate berries and milk while in captivity. Jacko wasn't fed any meat, out of fear that the taste of meat would turn the beast savage. Judging from the description in the original report, Jacko sounds like a young Sasquatch, not yet fully grown. He was 4 feet 7 inches (1.4 m) tall and approximately 127 pounds (57 kg). According to the *Daily Colonist*, Jacko resembled "a human being with one exception, his entire body, excepting his hand (or paws) and feet are covered with glossy hair about one inch [2.5 cm] long."

Much to the extreme frustration of Bigfoot researchers, who have spent countless hours poring through old newspapers looking for more information about this incident, no record remains of whatever happened to Jacko. At the time, there had been some talk of shipping the creature to London, England, for exhibit. Some people in the Yale area believed that Jacko was sent East by train

In his 1892 book *The Wilderness Hunter*, avid outdoorsman, conservationist, and amateur naturalist Theodore "Teddy" Roosevelt reported without any apparent skepticism a Bigfoot sighting he had heard about. The sighting had occurred near the Salmon River in Idaho. Roosevelt said he found this tale of "a great goblin-beast" "impressive."

but died in transit. Some skeptics have questioned whether the Jacko incident actually happened. If the *Victoria Daily Colonist* is to be believed, however, it remains the only documented account of a Bigfoot being captured alive.

That's No Teddy Bear!

The possibility of the existence of a Bigfoot-like creature received a huge boost in the late-nineteenth century from the testimony of one of the most revered figures in American history, celebrated for both his political savvy and his wilderness skills. The future U.S. president Theodore Roosevelt provided a secondhand account of an unusually violent Bigfoot encounter said to have occurred in a remote corner of Idaho sometime in the mid-1800s. In his book, *The Wilderness Hunter*, first published in 1892, "Teddy" Roosevelt told of a young fur trapper whom, after being stalked for day or two by a smelly, furry, bipedal creature, returned to his camp one evening to find his trapping partner dead, his neck broken and mauled. Wrote Roosevelt, "The footprints of the unknown beast-creature, printed deep in the soft soil, told the whole story."

CHAPTER 3

BIGFOOT EVIDENCE

According to the Bigfoot Field Researchers Organization (BFRO), which bills itself as the only scientific research organization exploring the Bigfoot/Sasquatch mystery, there have been 4,120 sightings of Bigfoot/Sasquatch/Yeti-type creatures worldwide. Three thousand seven hundred and eighty-six of these have occurred in the United States, with Washington (496 sightings) and California (424 sightings) leading the pack. Sightings have occurred in every state except Hawaii. There have been 266 sightings in Canada, with the majority (118) occurring in British Columbia. In addition, sightings have been reported in Malaysia (36), Australia (1), China (11), the Himalayan region (10), Indonesia (30), and Russia (2).

This still photo is taken from a 16mm film made by Ivan Marx in 1977. The film reportedly shows a Bigfoot creature roaming the forest near Bossburg, Washington. The film is now almost universally viewed as a hoax, and many believe Marx's wife, Peggy, donned a Bigfoot suit and performed for the camera.

Evidence for Bigfoot's existence breaks down into four basic categories: sightings, tracks, Native American myths and folklore, and one particularly tantalizing (and controversial) piece of film footage.

Sightings

Bigfoot sightings, of varying degrees of reliability, have occurred all over the United States and Canada. They are primarily concentrated in northern California, Washington State, Oregon, Alaska, and British Columbia. Mount St. Helens, site of the famous Ape Canyon incident in 1924, was once a hot spot for Sasquatch encounters, along with Bluff Creek, California, and the Blue Mountains near Walla Walla, Washington. More recently, Bigfoot hunters have concentrated their efforts on a particular region in Wyoming, located some-where between Cody and Yellowstone National Park. In addition, the Florida Everglades may also hide Bigfoot or perhaps one of his relatives.

Bigfoot sightings usually occur in remote areas with very low human populations and in places that have an annual rainfall of 20 inches (0.5 m). It should also be noted that most Bigfoot sightings occur in areas that also are home to bears. Skeptics have long suspected that Bigfoot encounters are nothing more than misapprehended bear sightings. Even some Bigfoot experts believe that 70 to 80 percent of all alleged sightings are either hoaxes or mistaken identification of other animals.

Many sightings take place at night, alongside lonely stretches of road at the fringes of civilization. Numerous eyewitnesses have reported that Bigfoot's eyes reflected light like those of a cat, appearing to glow red or yellow or green. A pungent and unpleasant odor emanates from the furry creature, a stench that is vividly recalled by almost everyone who encounters Bigfoot. Very rarely is more than one Sasquatch seen at a time and usually only for as long as it takes for the creature to disappear back into the murky shadows of the forest.

Tracks

Perhaps the most persuasive evidence of Bigfoot's presence is the gigantic footprints that inspired the creature's popular nickname. These are often more than 14 inches (0.3 m) long. The tracks, which resemble the impression of a bare human foot, are too large and wide to belong to a human being or even a gorilla (which only exist in captivity in North America). The prints also sink much deeper than any corresponding human footprints, seeming to confirm that they were left behind by something bigger and heavier than any ordinary human being. The prints are usually found in wet soil, soft earth, mud, or snow and have often been discovered not far from where Bigfoot sightings had previously occurred. The spacing of the tracks suggests that the creature has an enormous stride (more than 3 feet [0.9 m]), and that it can easily step over obstacles such as fences and boulders.

But are these tracks authentic? Although there have undeniably been numerous hoaxes, confusing the issue and prejudicing some people against the possibility that Sasquatches actually exist, Bigfoot experts believe that many of the giant footprints are genuine.

Careful analysis of the most credible and seemingly authentic tracks reveals an astonishing degree of detail. This includes impressions of realistic

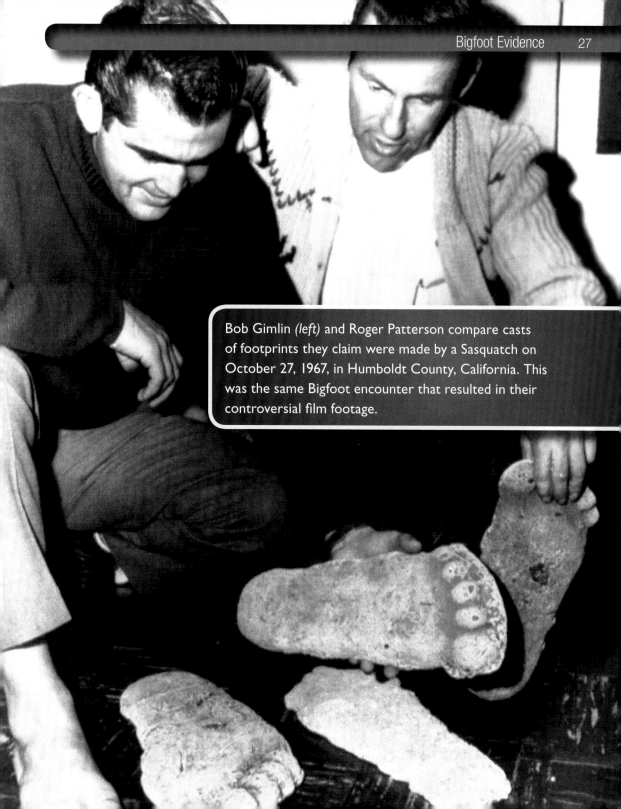

Bob Gimlin *(left)* and Roger Patterson compare casts of footprints they claim were made by a Sasquatch on October 27, 1967, in Humboldt County, California. This was the same Bigfoot encounter that resulted in their controversial film footage.

wrinkles and ridges—known as dermal ridges and akin to fingerprints—in the fleshy parts of the creature's feet. Many of these prints also feature a midtarsal break, which is a distinctive pattern formed when an ape's foot bends before taking the next stride. Human feet do not do this. Furthermore, subtle differences between human and Sasquatch footprints make sense anatomically, when Bigfoot's superior size and weight are taken into account. Anyone faking these tracks would have to possess an extensive knowledge of human and ape anatomy, as well as a thorough understanding of the physics of bipedal locomotion.

Yet it should be noted that mistakes can be made when examining these kinds of "footprints." Bear prints can often be mistaken for those of a Bigfoot. In addition, tightly clumped tracks of an animal or animals can appear to be a single large footprint. Any smaller footprints or tracks made in snow can begin to appear much larger and differently shaped as the snow melts.

Although footprints are the most common type of impression left behind by Bigfoot, other kinds of tracks have occasionally been found as well. Hand and knuckle prints, possibly created when a Sasquatch stumbled and/or began to rise from a sitting position, reveal that Bigfoot's hands are also larger and wider than an adult human's hands. The palm is broad and flat, and the fingers are stubby. These creatures also seem to lack an opposable thumb, something confirmed by a number of eyewitness reports.

In 2000, an expert team from the BFRO left fruit in the middle of a muddy portion of the Skookum Meadows area of Gifford Pinchot National Park in Washington State. The fruit served as bait, and some kind of animal was drawn to it and left its impression in the mud. The BFRO team made casts of this impression. They concluded that the impression revealed the forearm, hip, thigh, heel, ankle, and Achilles tendon of a Bigfoot. Some Bigfoot experts agreed, while others thought it more likely that the impression was made by an elk. Elk hoof and coyote paw prints appear in the cast, and both elk and bear hair were also detected. Yet a retired biomedical researcher analyzed this hair and claimed it was from a single creature, which he believed to be a Sasquatch. He admitted, however, that there was no way to test or prove this claim.

Indigenous Myths or Early Encounters?: Sasquatch and the First Peoples

The indigenous peoples of North America have known of Bigfoot for countless generations. The myths and folklore of numerous Northwest Indian tribes are full of stories about large, smelly, hairy giants who dwell in the hills and forests, apart from humanity. These creatures go by many names—Sesquac, Seatco, Tsiatko, Dsonqua, Sokquatl, and more—but often bear a striking resemblance to the modern and popular conception of Bigfoot.

Bigfoot-like creatures can also be found on totem poles, pottery, and other Indian artifacts. Particularly intriguing are several prehistoric stone heads that were found along the shores of the Columbia River, between Oregon and Washington State. Although little is known about the people who carved these heads hundreds of years ago, the chiseled stones feature distinctly ape-like faces. Ancient Northwest Indians should have had no knowledge of any primate except man. With no exposure to chimps or gorillas or even monkeys, whom could these forgotten sculptors have been trying to depict except Sasquatch?

The Patterson-Gimlin Film

Perhaps the most famous, controversial, and hotly debated piece of evidence for the existence of Bigfoot is 952 frames of color film footage shot by a man named Roger Patterson in Bluff Creek, California, in October 1967. The footage appears to show a full-grown Sasquatch striding confidently along a sunlit creek bed littered with fallen timber and other debris from the stream. At one point, the Bigfoot, which is covered with dark black fur, looks back at the filmmaker before walking farther away, at. At this point, the camera ran out of film.

Bigfoot tracks had often been found in this region of northern California, including some discovered earlier that summer. Patterson and his friend Bob Gimlin had been searching for Bigfoot on horseback when they supposedly stumbled onto the creature at Bluff Creek. Following the filming and after losing track of the immense black figure in the woods, Patterson and Gimlin made casts of the creature's footprints, which were over 2 feet (0.6 m) long.

The brief snippet of footage filmed by Patterson and Gimlin, which runs slightly less than two minutes, has been analyzed and argued about for more

This still photo is taken from the October 1967 film taken by Roger Patterson and Bob Gimlin that purports to show Bigfoot roaming the forests of northern California.

than four decades. Although it has frequently been dismissed as a hoax, this has never been proved, and many experts continue to vouch for its authenticity.

A persistent rumor exists that the "Bigfoot" in the film is actually an actor wearing a costume created by John Chambers, a famous Hollywood makeup artist. Chambers won an Academy Award for his work on the original *Planet of the Apes* movies (the first film in the series was released in 1968). However, Chambers denied any involvement in the incident. He did once create a large stone Bigfoot prop designed for use in a carnival, as well as a giant Iceman that was displayed at midwestern state fairs. But he claimed to not have known Patterson and Gimlin at the time of their filming. He further claimed that he was a good makeup artist but not good enough to create something as convincing as the creature that appears in the Patterson-Gimlin film. Many people have also pointed out that the actors in the *Planet of the Apes* films are not dressed in full ape suits, but are merely wearing prosthetic hands and masks that cover the head, face, and neck.

If the Patterson-Gimlin footage is indeed genuine, as many serious Bigfoot researchers believe it to be, then this precious footage provides us with our best glimpse yet of what Bigfoot truly looks like.

Other Documentary Evidence

The highly disputed Patterson-Gimlin film is not the only purported visual or documentary evidence for the existence of Bigfoot. Several other films and

BIGFOOT'S LINKS TO HOLLYWOOD MAKEUP ARTISTS

The John Chambers rumor is believed to have been started by the Hollywood director John Landis, best known for the movies *Animal House*, *The Blues Brothers*, and the Michael Jackson video "Thriller." Landis and Chambers both worked on *Beneath the Planet of the Apes* in 1973. In that same year, Landis hired Chambers for a bit part in *Schlock*, Landis's first directing job, a comedy about a Bigfoot-like creature that terrorizes college students. Rick Baker, a student of John Chambers, created the ape-man costume and makeup for *Schlock*, and he would later create the Bigfoot costume and makeup for the movie *Harry and the Hendersons* (1987). He would also work on the 1976 *King Kong* remake, *Greystoke: The Legend of Tarzan, Lord of the Apes* (1984), *Werewolf* (1987), *Gorillas in the Mist* (1988), *Missing Link* (1988), *Wolf* (1994), the 2001 remake of *Planet of the Apes*, and *The Wolfman* (2010).

photographs exist and have been released to the public, though none offers controversy-free, indisputable proof. In addition, audio recordings have been made of apelike calls purported to belong to Bigfoot, though analysis of these has been inconclusive.

Cryptozoologist Paul Freeman was already renowned for his discovery of Bigfoot tracks featuring dermal ridges and his sighting of an 8-foot (2.4 m) tall, reddish-brown Sasquatch. Yet in 1994, he achieved even greater fame and notoriety when he captured images of a large, hairy creature appearing to walk upright in the Blue Mountains of Washington State. Some experts declared the footage authentic, while others said the resolution was too low to draw any firm conclusions. Freeman died in 2003. His footage is readily available on the Internet.

During a 1996 fishing trip at Chopaka Lake in Washington State, Lori Pate and her family members twice sighted a large, apelike creature walking on two feet. The third sighting was captured on film, as the supposed Bigfoot runs across a hill and then walks into a group of trees. Later forensic tests and measurements concluded that this creature was about 5 feet tall (1.6 m), had a leg length of 2.5 feet (0.76m), was running at about 8.5 miles per hour (13.8 km/hr), and had a stride of 4.25 feet (1.3 m). This video was examined, dissected, and discussed in the 2003 documentary *Sasquatch: Legend Meets Science*, aired by the Discovery Channel. Pate's footage is also widely available on the Internet.

Northwest Pennsylvania has not been a traditional hotspot of Bigfoot sightings. Yet in 2007 a man named Rick Jacobs photographed what he and the BFRO described as a juvenile Bigfoot. Hoping only to photograph deer, Jacobs sprinkled an aromatic deer attractant mix at the base of a tree. The bait worked, and Jacobs photographed both deer and bear cubs that wandered to the site to investigate the smell. Yet so, too, did an unidentifiable creature that was about the size of an adolescent bear, with dark fur covering its entire body, but with a more apelike anatomy. In the photos, the creature appears to press its face to the ground to smell the mixture. This posture echoes more closely the way an ape would bend to smell the earth than the way a bear would. Yet officials from the Pennsylvania Game Commission confidently declared that this mysterious apelike creature was merely a young, skinny bear with mange, a skin disease that can result in some hair loss.

CHAPTER 4

OTHER MYSTERIOUS APE-MEN

Bigfoot is not the only mysterious anthropoid reputed to prowl the Earth. Sightings and evidence of shaggy Wild Men and man-apes occur all over the world, in almost every culture and country.

The Yeti

Beyond a doubt, Bigfoot's most famous relative is the Yeti, also known as the Abominable Snowman. Said to live in the snowy peaks of the Himalayan Mountains, the Yeti is occasionally glimpsed by explorers and mountain climbers attempting to scale Mount Everest or one of the other surrounding

A Tibetan man holds what is said to be the scalp of a Yeti. The scalp was housed in a Buddhist monastery in Pangboche, Tibet. Tests on hair samples taken from it were inconclusive. An alleged Yeti hand was stolen from this same monastery in 1959.

peaks. Its bare footprints have also been discovered from time to time, sunken deep into the stark white snow. Like Bigfoot, the Yeti is well known to its region's indigenous population, in this case the people of Tibet and Nepal. The Yeti has deep roots in Tibetan and Nepalese religion and folklore. In fact, the name "Yeti" comes from the Sherpa term *yet-the*, which can be loosely translated as "that thing."

The mountain-dwelling monster did not become world-famous, however, until 1921, when members of a British expedition to Mount Everest spotted dimly seen figures moving high upon the mountain slopes. At that same high elevation spot, the explorers later found a set of large, unexplained footprints. A Calcutta newspaper reported the incident, referring to the unknown creature as the Abominable Snowman. This was nothing more than a mistranslation of another Sherpa phrase, which actually meant something like "man-sized snow creature." The more colorful name quickly caught on with the public, however, and the story of the Abominable Snowman soon spread across the planet.

Since then, several expeditions have set out in search of the Yeti, while others have attempted (unsuccessfully) to debunk the legend. One popular theory holds that the Snowman does not actually live in the mountains themselves, but in the secluded jungle valleys between the peaks, only occasionally crossing the frozen slopes to get from one temperate valley to another. So far the Yeti's existence has been neither proved nor disproved, although mountaineers still occasionally report seeing a mysterious figure amid the endless snow or find inexplicable tracks high in the mountains.

The Yeti and Sasquatch are closely linked in the public imagination. In fact, Bigfoot has often been described as "the Abominable Snowman of

America." But, aside from the fact that they both leave puzzling footprints, there's no strong reason to assume that they belong to the same species of unknown hominid. Although the Yeti is rarely seen close up and eyewitness reports vary, the mountain creature sounds smaller than the average Bigfoot. Some researchers believe that the Yeti more closely resembles an orangutan than a Sasquatch, although it is impossible to know for sure. Since the forbidding peaks of the Himalayas are even harder and more dangerous to explore than the densest North American forests, the mystery of the Abominable Snowman is not likely to be solved anytime soon.

The Skunk Ape

Closer to home, the Florida Skunk Ape may or may not be a separate and distinct species of Bigfoot found throughout the South, including North Carolina and Arkansas. The majority of sightings, however, have occurred in the Florida Keys and Everglades. Like the Sasquatch of the Pacific Northwest, the Skunk Ape is a smelly, apelike creature whose actual existence remains not only unproved but also unacknowledged by modern science. The Skunk Ape is said to have a strong and unpleasant odor that has offended the nostrils of just about every witness who ever encountered the semimythical creature. The creature first gained widespread notoriety during the 1970s, although there are scattered accounts of its presence dating back much further. Some theories state that its characteristic noxious odor is a defense mechanism. In order to keep people away, the Skunk Ape may roll in dead carcasses to pick up a putrid smell.

Is the Skunk Ape simply a southern variety of Bigfoot, or a different kind of anthropoid altogether? That depends on whom you ask. Some eyewitnesses describe a tall, bipedal primate much like a traditional Sasquatch, who, it should be recalled, is also usually described as being extremely foul smelling. Other sightings, however, seem to involve a much smaller and more apelike creature, comparable to a chimpanzee or small orangutan. Some noted cryptozoologists, such as Loren Coleman, author of numerous books on the subject, believe that there may actually be two separate types of unknown primates lurking within the lush foliage of the Florida Everglades.

In any event, sightings of some kind of Skunk Ape continue to this day. As recently as December 2000, two intriguing color photos were mailed anonymously to the sheriff's department in Sarasota, Florida. They were accompanied by a letter from a woman. The letter writer claimed she took these photos from her backyard after an apelike creature that she believed to be an orangutan had taken apples from a basket on her porch. The eye-catching pictures capture two views of a shaggy, gray-haired creature with a silvery beard. Two red eyes reflect the glare of the flashbulbs. Although partially concealed behind a leafy shrub, the monster in the photos does look something like an adult male orangutan, especially around the face.

Chupacabra

Springing from Latin American folklore traditions, the Chupacabra, which is Spanish for "goat sucker," is said to be about the size of a small bear, with a row of sharp, quill-like spines running from its neck to its tail. Rather than

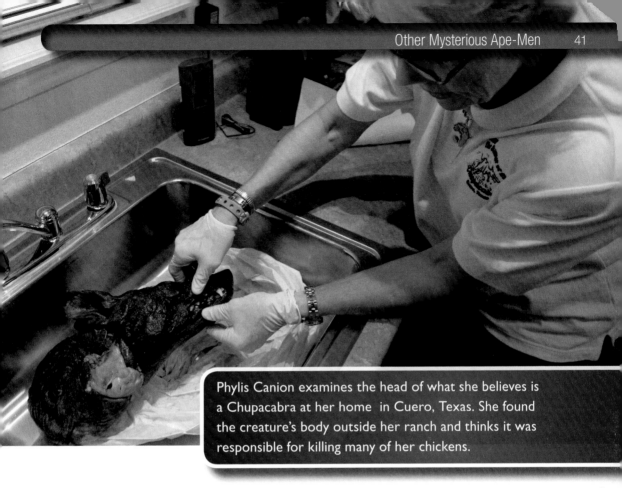

Phylis Canion examines the head of what she believes is a Chupacabra at her home in Cuero, Texas. She found the creature's body outside her ranch and thinks it was responsible for killing many of her chickens.

being hairy, it is often described as leathery or scaly, with greenish-gray skin. Witnesses more often describe it as reptilian rather than apelike. Yet it is also doglike in some respects, with a canine-type nose and face and large fangs and claws. It is often said to have a forked tongue and hisses or screeches when agitated. Like Bigfoot and the Skunk Ape, Chupacabra is most remembered for its terrible smell, in this case the stench of rotten eggs.

Accounts and sightings of Chupacabra seem to have originated in Puerto Rico but have since spread throughout the Caribbean, Central America, South America, the United States (from Texas to Maine), and even to Russia

BIGFOOT HOAXES

Even some cryptozoologists who are inclined to believe in at least the possibility of the existence of Bigfoot claim that the vast majority of sightings are
either misidentifications of other animals, like bears, or are outright hoaxes.
The deliberate and staged filming of a Bigfoot "sighting," the fabrication of footprints, or the phony discovery of fake Bigfoot hair or even an entire Bigfoot
carcass is not only a violation of the truth, it also muddies the scientific picture.
Hoaxes make it that much harder to arrive at firm conclusions regarding the
existence of Sasquatch. They call into question the value of seemingly authentic
evidence and the reliability of all Bigfoot eyewitnesses and "experts."

The credibility of Bigfoot studies and the science behind it is particularly
undermined when hoaxes are devised by prominent members of the Bigfoot
research community. One such case is alleged to have occurred in 2005, when
Tom Biscardi, the CEO of Searching for Bigfoot, Inc., a for-profit organization
that claims to investigate eyewitness accounts of Bigfoot encounters, made several appearances on a paranormal-themed, nationally syndicated radio show.
During one radio interview, he claimed that his group was tracking a Bigfoot in
California and that a capture was imminent. In a later appearance,
he claimed to have access to a captured Bigfoot and
was arranging for a public viewing of it via pay-per-
view television. Finally, in yet another radio

interview, he claimed that he had been duped and that there was no captured Bigfoot. The community of Bigfoot enthusiasts generally believe that Biscardi, far from being duped, was the one fabricating the entire story.

An even more outlandish hoax was perpetrated three years later and captured the world's attention, thanks to the new media phenomenon You-Tube. An amateur video shot by Rick Dyer and Matthew Whitton purporting to show a deceased Bigfoot found in northern Georgia went viral soon after it was posted. Ironically, Tom Biscardi was brought in to provide an "independent" investigation. He also paid Dyer and Whitton $50,000. Upon closer inspection of the carcass, however, it was discovered that the hair was fake, the head was hollow, and the feet were made of plastic. Dyer and Whiton were forced to admit their perpetration of a hoax. Biscardi's exact role in the events remains unclear, as does what he knew and when he knew it.

and the Philippines. This dog-reptile hybrid drains the blood of its animal victims—mostly chickens, sheep, cattle, and other livestock—leaving behind triangular puncture marks.

Theories about what this creature may actually be have included coyote-dog hybrids, mutated coyotes, and coyotes infected with parasites and mange. In 2010, a University of Michigan researcher concluded definitively that all Chupacabras that had been sighted were almost certainly coyotes infected with a parasite popularly known as scabies. A scabies infection would lead to fur loss, toughened skin, and a putrid smell.

Other Notable Ape-Men

The Yeti and the Skunk Ape are only two of the most notable anthropoids believed to be hiding in the world's diverse wilderness regions. In mainland China, the mysterious Yeren, a shaggy, red-haired wild man, has been the subject of extensive research and speculation. Unfortunately, when it comes to acquiring definitive proof of the Yeren's existence, Chinese cryptozoologists have not had any better luck than their North American counterparts. The true nature of the Yeren remains unknown. Yet in 2010, reports surfaced

During a news conference, Bigfoot hunter Tom Biscardi holds a photo of what he claims to be the mouth and teeth of a deceased Bigfoot found in northern Georgia by two local men. The discovery was later proved to be a hoax.

that a team of Chinese researchers at the Shennongjia Nature Reserve were examining unidentified hair believed to be from a Yeren, often referred to in North America as Hubei Bigfoot.

Meanwhile, Russian scholars speak of the Almas of Mongolia, who may or may not be the last surviving remnants of our Neanderthal cousins. On the continent of Australia, there are occasional sightings of a Yowie, which sounds an awful lot like a Sasquatch—except that it only has four toes on each foot. And cryptozoologists are still searching the jungles of Sumatra for the Orang-Pendek, a 5-foot-tall (1.5 m), bipedal primate. Even skeptics who scoff at Bigfoot and the Yeti concede that the Orang-Pendek probably exists.

How all of these creatures relate to Bigfoot remains to be discovered. But it's worth remembering, once again, that early humans are known to have coexisted with *Gigantopithecus*, the Neanderthals, and many other prehistoric manlike creatures. What's more, many of these manlike beings survived for millions of years before (supposedly) becoming extinct. Given that *Homo sapiens* have existed for only about fifty thousand years, just a tiny sliver of time in the ongoing evolution of hominids, we should not be too surprised to find out that we're not really as unique as we think we are.

CHAPTER 5

BIGFOOT GOES POP!

Regardless of whether Sasquatch really exists, Bigfoot is undeniably alive and well in the alternate universe of pop culture. Though the creature's celebrity heyday may have been in the 1970s and '80s, Bigfoot has long outpaced its fifteen minutes of fame. Sasquatch and similar man-ape creatures, traditional figures of indigenous folklore, would seem to have evolved into permanent fixtures in global culture. Its ongoing currency within and relevance to consumer culture, in particular, ensures that the vast majority of Bigfoot "sightings" occur on our television, computer, and movie screens, as well as in the pages of our comic books, novels, and supermarket tabloids.

The cast of the television show *Harry and the Hendersons* pose for pictures in Los Angeles, California.

Movies and Television

Since the early 1970s, more than thirty-five major films have been released that feature a Bigfoot story. These range from action dramas and horror movies to comedies and spoofs. Perhaps the best known of these is the 1987 family comedy-drama *Harry and the Hendersons*, which spawned a spin-off television sitcom. One of the popular and critical favorites of the 2011 Sundance Film Festival was a movie called *Letters from the Big Man*. It concerns a government hydrologist who travels to Oregon to conduct a stream survey. Once there, she encounters and develops a relationship with a Sasquatch.

In many ways, Bigfoot first entered the general public's consciousness through television, and the creature continues to flourish there today. Most North Americans first "encountered" Bigfoot through quasi-documentary, cryptozoological investigative television programs like *In Search of...*, hosted by Leonard Nimoy (*Star Trek*'s Mr. Spock). Bigfoot became a sensation among young people when the creature, enhanced by bionic technology, had a recurring role on the popular 1970s action show *The Six Million Dollar Man* and its spin-off *The Six Million Dollar Woman*. Today, Bigfoot continues to appear regularly on popular investigative documentaries airing on the History Channel, Discovery, Animal Planet, and A&E, among other cable networks.

Online Video, Games, and Toys

Bigfoot is not only a star of the silver screen and an enduring television personality. The creature has also become a cyber-celebrity, daily appearing on personal computer screens worldwide. When Bigfoot's name is typed into YouTube's search engine, more than sixty-two thousand results appear, and new videos are added every day. These run the gamut from earnest amateur sightings and famous footage like the Patterson-Gimlin film to clever hoaxes, over-the-top comedic spoofs, mockumentaries, and film trailers.

Bigfoot has also become a popular character in video and computer games. In most of these games, Bigfoot has only a cameo role or can be a playable character (as in *The Simpsons, Tony Hawk's Underground 2,* and the *Darkstalkers* series). Yet in some, like *Sam and Max Hit the Road,* the game centers upon the search for and attempted recapture of a Bigfoot escaped from a carnival.

In the more analog 1970s and '80s, Bigfoot inspired board games, pinball machines, action figures, store-bought Halloween costumes, and lunch boxes. There were even Bigfoot snowshoes, guaranteed to leave behind massive footprints in the snow. While these products are no longer manufactured, they remain hot commodities among collectors, who engage in heated and high-priced bidding wars for them on auction Web sites like eBay.

Comic Books, Graphic Novels, and Other Fiction

The ordinarily highly elusive Sasquatch is frequently spotted among the pages of comic books, graphic novels and graphic nonfiction, and traditional novels.

Squatch, the Bigfoot mascot of the Seattle SuperSonics, entertains the crowd during an NBA game at ARCO Arena in Sacramento, California.

The creature also routinely makes headlines in sensationalistic supermarket tabloids like the *National Inquirer* and the *Weekly World News*.

Bigfoot is the star of his own comic book series titled *Proof*. In it, Bigfoot actually works as a sort of cryptozoologist. In conjunction with a secret government agency, he searches for other mysterious creatures, including Chupacabra, jackalopes, dinosaurs, and fairies.

In the four-comic book series *Savage*, Bigfoot is revealed to be a man who transforms into a beast. This transformative ability can be passed from one man to another, and the resulting Bigfoot creature is charged with protecting humanity from danger, in this case a terrorizing pack of werewolves.

A more sinister man-Bigfoot transformation is achieved by the Marvel Comics character Dr. Walter Langkowski. Due to gamma radiation experiments gone bad, he has the ability to transform into an orange-furred, astoundingly powerful creature who calls himself Sasquatch. He is largely immune to injury, has sharp claws and teeth, and can leap vast distances. He frequently both battles against and joins forces with the various X-Men, the Hulk, and other Marvel superheroes.

Numerous young adult novels feature Bigfoot, including Eric S. Brown's *Bigfoot War*, in which a young man seeks to avenge the murder of his family by a Sasquatch, and Dallas Tanner's *Track of the Bigfoot*, in which a childhood encounter with Bigfoot leads to the protagonist's later scientific search for the creature. In addition, hundreds of nonfiction titles about Bigfoot and the search for the creature are available. Some of the more intriguing include *Enoch: A Bigfoot Story* by Autumn Williams; *Impossible Visits: The Inside Story of Interactions with Sasquatch at Habituation Sites* by Christopher Noel; *Valley of the Skookum:*

SASQUATCH XING

Bigfoot and Sasquatch crossing signs are not uncommon throughout the Pacific Northwest, including along the remote roadways of northern California, Oregon, and Washington State.

Four Years of Encounters with Bigfoot by Sali Sheppard-Wolford; *Sasquatch: Legend Meets Science* by Jeff Meldrum; *Bigfoot!: The True Story of Apes in America* by Loren Coleman; and *Bigfoot Observer's Field Manual: A Practical and Easy-to-Follow Step-by-Step Guide to Your Very Own Face-to-Face Encounter with a Legend* by Robert W. Morgan.

Advertising and Marketing

Over the years, Bigfoot has become an influential celebrity pitchman, lending his name and image to a wide range of products, including campers, monster trucks, beer, wine, gas stations, skateboards, skis, pizzas, an Internet search engine, computer hard drives, and even beef jerky. In fact, the company behind the Jack Link's brand of beef jerky has run a series of commercials in which various outdoorsmen play practical jokes on Bigfoot, sending the creature into a murderous rage.

Numerous tourist attractions, primarily in the Pacific Northwest, use the Bigfoot/Sasquatch name and image to promote restaurants, motels, gift shops, and amusement parks. Sasquatch has even been used as a sports mascot. Quatchi, a young Canadian Sasquatch, was a mascot for the 2010 Vancouver Winter Olympics, and Squatch is the Bigfoot mascot for the professional Seattle SuperSonics basketball team.

The Bigfoot Lurking Within

In the end, it hardly matters whether Bigfoot, Sasquatch, the Yeti, the Skunk Ape, and other mysterious and elusive ape-men continue to lurk in the world's

PARTY ANIMAL

Sasquatch has even become associated with several major festivals. The annual Sasquatch! Music Festival is held over Memorial Day weekend at an outdoor amphitheater in George, Washington. It features some of the most highly regarded indie, alternative, and hip-hop musical artists, as well as dance crews and comedy acts. There are four stages: the Bigfoot Stage, the Yeti Stage, the Sasquatch! Main Stage, and the Rumpus Room. In 2010, the festival included My Morning Jacket, Public Enemy, Vampire Weekend, MGMT, Band of Horses, She & Him, The National, OK Go, Pavement, LCD Soundsystem, the Dirty Projectors, Edward Sharpe and the Magnetic Zeros, The Hold Steady, and dozens of other acts.

The town of Willow Creek, California, self-proclaimed capital of "Bigfoot Country" and near the spot where the first casts of a Sasquatch footprint were made in 1958, hosts an annual Bigfoot Days festival over the Labor Day weekend. Kicking off with a parade led by Bigfoot himself, the festival also includes a car show, live bands, food and craft booths, and an ice cream social at the Willow Creek–China Flat Museum. The most prominent feature of this museum is a Bigfoot exhibition that includes Bigfoot pictures and footprint casts, maps, other Bigfoot-related papers and documents, and a research center.

remaining dense forests, swamps, and mountain valleys or merely in our fevered imaginations. The point is not whether they are surviving remnants of a primeval past or simply projections of our primal fears, whether they are wild creatures roaming free or only creations of admen and hucksters seeking to dupe the gullible and make a quick buck. What does matter is our interest in the possibility that such a creature exists and our desire to believe it is true. Modern humans—logical, civilized, and technologically advanced—have a powerful need to believe that there are still mysteries to be solved, pristine wildernesses to discover and previously unknown and unimagined creatures to encounter.

Twenty-first century humans, living highly denatured, digital lives still have a powerful need to experience the primal—the shaggy, dirty, smelly, uncivilized, wild, animalistic natures that continue to root and roost within each of us. For no matter how advanced our technology becomes, how sleek our cities, how comfortable and antiseptic our existence, we remain, at heart, animals, barely domesticated and struggling to survive. Each of us contains a wild man or woman whom we must control, confine, and contain in order to exist and succeed in the civilized world. Yet this wild creature continues to lurk within us and, under pressure, can burst out of its shackles at a moment's notice. In some ways, we have indeed encountered Bigfoot face-to-face, and Bigfoot is us.

GLOSSARY

anthropoid A creature resembling a human; the term is usually applied to the higher apes, such as the chimpanzee, gorilla, orangutan, and gibbon.

Bigfoot Popular nickname for a mysterious apelike creature believed to live deep in the forests of North America. The term, inspired by the large tracks discovered in Humboldt County, California, was first used by the *Humboldt Times* in 1958.

biped Any animal who walks on two feet, including humans and Bigfoot, if such a creature exists.

cryptid Any mysterious or legendary creature whose existence is not yet accepted or proved by modern science, such as Bigfoot, the Yeti (or Abominable Snowman), the Loch Ness monster, etc.

cryptozoology The study of mystery animals whose existence has been reported but not yet scientifically proved.

genus and species All living things can be classified according to their characteristics, into increasingly smaller and specific categories. The names for these categories, in order of increasing specificity, are: kingdom, phylum, class, order, family, genus, species. As far as we know, Bigfoot can be classified as follows: animal, vertebrate, mammal, primate. We don't yet know enough about Bigfoot to safely place his family, genus, and species.

Gigantopithecus blacki An immense prehistoric primate, possibly the largest ever, known to have lived in Asia between five hundred thousand and one million years ago. Often suggested as a possible ancestor of both Bigfoot and the Yeti, or Abominable Snowman.

hominid Members of the biological family *Hominidae*, including all species of two-legged primates, extinct and living.

hominoid Members of the larger superfamily *Hominoidae*, including humans, great apes, and gibbons. Not to be confused with hominid (see above).

Paranthropus A genus of prehistoric hominids who lived in Africa somewhere between one to three million years ago, including *Paranthropus aethiopicus*, *P. boisei*, and *P. robustus*. Some paleontologists lump *Paranthropus* in with another group of prehistoric hominids, *Australopithecus*, while other experts argue that they deserve a genus of their own. *Paranthropus* is viewed by some as a possible ancestor of Bigfoot.

primate A specific order of mammals with especially flexible hands and feet, each with five digits. Includes humans, apes, monkeys, and lemurs. Bigfoot, if such a creature exists, is almost certainly a primate.

sagittal crest A bony ridge running lengthwise across the top of the skull, between the right and left halves of the skull. It's exhibited by male gorillas and orangutans, some female gorillas, and, possibly, Bigfoot.

Sasquatch Another name for Bigfoot, loosely derived from *Sesquac* and other similar-sounding Canadian Indian terms. Coined in the 1920s by a Canadian journalist, J. W. Burns, to label the large, hairy giants described in the myths and folklore of First Nation Canadian tribes. Now used more or less interchangeably with "Bigfoot."

FOR MORE INFORMATION

International Cryptozoology Museum

661 Congress Street

Portland, ME 04104

(207) 518-9496

Web site: http://www.cryptozoologymuseum.com

Billed as the world's only fully public cryptozoology museum, the exhibits include an 8-foot (2.4 m) tall, 400-pound (181 kg) Bigfoot, a mermaid, a thunderbird, and other "mysteries of the world."

OregonBigfoot.com

P.O. Box 24332

Eugene, OR 97402

Web site: http://www.oregonbigfoot.com

OregonBigfoot.com is not a research organization, but rather a community of incidental Bigfoot witnesses, long-term witnesses, independent investigators, and those with a keen interest in this subject. Its members hail from all parts of the United States and across the world, and have created one of the largest databases of Bigfoot sightings and other Bigfoot-related information.

Ripley's Believe It or Not! Times Square

234 West 42nd Street

New York, NY 10036

(212) 398-3133

Web site: http://www.ripleysnewyork.com

For over forty years, Robert Ripley traveled the world collecting the unbeliev-
able, the inexplicable, and the one-of-a-kind. His vast collections are now
on display, including hundreds of weird and unusual artifacts.

Sasquatch Information Society

P.O. Box 48333

Seattle, WA 98148

Web site: http://www.bigfootinfo.org

This is a database containing Bigfoot news, articles, links, polls, events, sightings, interviews, and research.

Sasquatch Investigations of the Rockies, Inc.

P.O. Box 4566

Parker, CO 80134

Web site: http://www.sasquatchinvestigations.org

Sasquatch Investigations of the Rockies is a Bigfoot research group based in
Parker, Colorado. The purpose of the organization is to spend as much
time as possible in the target areas of the Rocky Mountains document-
ing the legendary Bigfoot/Sasquatch. The group's most compelling data to
date is available on its Web site.

Searching for Bigfoot, Inc.

1134 Crane Street, Suite 216

Menlo Park, CA 94025

(650) 566-4001

Web site: http://www.searchingforbigfoot.com

This organization purports to investigate eyewitness accounts of Bigfoot
    sightings.

Texas Bigfoot Research Conservancy (TBRC)

P.O. Box 866621

Plano, TX 75086-6621

(877) 529-5550

Web site: http://www.texasbigfoot.org

The TBRC is a nonprofit scientific research organization comprised of vol-
    unteer investigators, scientists, and naturalists who pursue education and
    research activities pertaining to the centuries-old "wildman" or "hairy man"
    phenomenon in North America. The TBRC proposes that the source of
    the phenomenon is a biological entity, probably an unlisted large primate.
    The organization is engaged in activities designed to test that hypothesis.

Web Sites

Due to the changing nature of Internet links, Rosen Publishing has developed
an online list of Web sites related to the subject of this book. This site is
updated regularly. Please use this link to access the list:

http://www.rosenlinks.com/me/big

FOR FURTHER READING

Arment, Chad. *The Historical Bigfoot*. Lancaster County, PA: Coachwhip
Publications, 2006.

Bader, Christopher D., F. Carson Mencken, and Joseph O. Baker. *Paranormal
America: Ghost Encounters, UFO Sightings, Bigfoot Hunts, and Other Curiosities
in Religion and Culture*. New York, NY: NYU Press, 2011.

Brown, Eric S. *Bigfoot War*. Winnipeg, MN, Canada: Coscom Entertainment, 2010.

Budd, Deena West. *The Weiser Guide to Cryptozoology: Werewolves, Dragons,
Skyfish, Lizard Men, and Other Fascinating Creatures Real and Mysterious*. San
Francisco, CA: Weiser Books, 2010.

Buhs, Joshua Blu. *Bigfoot: The Life and Times of a Legend*. Chicago, IL: University
of Chicago Press, 2010.

Childress, David Hatcher. *Yetis, Sasquatch, and Hairy Giants*. Kempton, IL:
Adventures Unlimited Press, 2010.

Hobday, Lance A. *Supposedly True Stories of Bigfoot Sightings*. Charleston, SC:
CreateSpace, 2010.

Matthews, Rupert. *Sasquatch: True-Life Encounters with Legendary Ape-Men*.
Edison, NJ: Chartwell Books, 2008.

McLeod, Michael. *Anatomy of a Beast: Obsession and Myth on the Trail of
Bigfoot*. Berkeley, CA: University of California Press, 2009.

Meldrum, Jeff. *Sasquatch: Legend Meets Science*. New York, NY: Forge
Books, 2007.

Morgan, Robert W. *Bigfoot Observer's Field Manual: A Practical and Easy-to-
Follow Step-by-Step Guide to Your Very Own Face-to-Face Encounter with a
Legend*. Ravensdale, WA: Pine Woods Press, 2008.

Noel, Christopher. *Impossible Visits: The Inside Story of Interactions with Sasquatch at Habituation Sites*. Bloomington, IN: Xlibris Corporation, 2009.

Paulides, David. *The Hoopa Project: Bigfoot Encounters in California*. Blaine, WA: Hancock House, 2008.

Sheppard-Wolford, Sali. *Valley of the Skookum: Four Years of Encounters with Bigfoot*. Ravensdale, WA: Pine Woods Press, 2006.

Tanner, Dallas. *Track of the Bigfoot*. Charleston, SC: CreateSpace, 2008.

Townsend, John. *Bigfoot and Other Mysterious Creatures*. New York, NY: Crabtree Publishing, 2008.

Wells, Jeffrey. *Bigfoot in Georgia*. Ravensdale, WA: Pine Woods Press, 2010.

Williams, Autumn. *Enoch: A Bigfoot Story*. Charleston, SC: CreateSpace, 2010.

INDEX

About the Authors

Stewart Cowley is a writer who lives in Vero Beach, Florida.

Greg Cox grew up in Bigfoot country—the Pacific Northwest. He is the author of numerous books relating to science fiction, fantasy, superheroes, and unexplained mysteries.

Photo Credits

Cover, back cover, p. 1 Andrew Rich/Vetta/Getty Images; cover (background), back cover, pp. 1, 6, 12–13, 16, 19, 23, 33, 36, 42–43, 46, 54 Shutterstock; cover, back cover, p. 1 (camera lens) © www.istockhoto.com/jsemeniuk; p. 5 © Dale O'Dell/Alamy; pp. 7, 24, 27, 41 © AP Images; p. 10 Forrest Anderson/ Time & Life Pictures/Getty Images; p. 14 Bill O'Leary/The Washington Post via Getty Images; pp. 17, 31 © Fortean/Topham/The Image Works; p. 21 Library of Congress Prints and Photographs Division; p. 37 Popperfoto/Getty Images; p. 44 Ian Sherr/AFP/Getty Images; p. 47 Darlene Hammond/Archive Photos/ Getty Images; p. 50 Rocky Widner/NBAE via Getty Images; p. 52 C. McIntyre/ PhotoLink/Photodisc/Getty Images.

Designer: Matthew Cauli; Photo Researcher: Amy Feinberg